BookLife
PUBLISHING

©2022
BookLife Publishing Ltd.
King's Lynn
Norfolk, PE30 4LS

All rights reserved.
Printed in Poland.

A catalogue record for
this book is available from
the British Library.

ISBN: 978-1-83927-450-3

Written by:
Madeline Tyler

Edited by:
Emilie Dufresne

Designed by:
Drue Rintoul

Photo Credits

CONTENTS

Words that look like this can be found in the glossary on page 24.

IN THE SKIES

The skies are full of lots of different animals. From big birds to tiny bugs, flying animals can be found all around the world.

Let's meet the animal champions that call the skies their home!

WHAT MAKES AN ANIMAL CHAMPION?

Animal champions don't always have to be the biggest, fastest, or strongest animals around. They are special because of the <u>adaptations</u> they have, or things they can do.

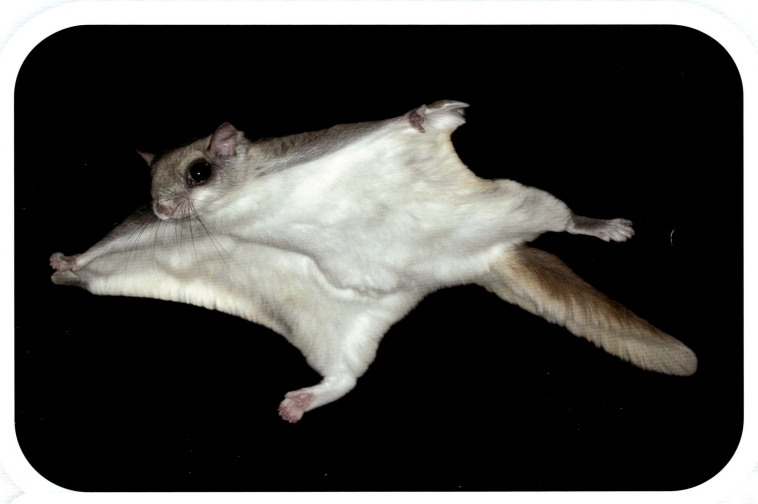

Come on! Let's head into the skies...

PEREGRINE FALCON

Peregrine falcons can be found in lots of different <u>habitats</u> — from cliffs by the sea to tall buildings in cities.

Champion of Catching

Talons

Peregrine falcons have sharp talons that help them catch their main <u>prey</u> – other birds.

Peregrine falcons hunt their prey by diving! While flying in the air, they spot their prey and dive down at them. They can reach speeds of over 300 kilometres per hour when diving.

Champion of the Dive

They grab prey out of the air with their talons.

COMMON VAMPIRE BAT

Bats can fly like birds, but they are <u>mammals</u>. Vampire bats are <u>nocturnal</u> and hunt at night. They have sharp teeth that they use to bite their prey's skin.

A vampire bat's nose can <u>sense</u> heat and help it to find its favourite food – blood!

Champion of Sucking Blood

Vampire bats find their way around in the dark using echolocation. They make noises that bounce off walls, trees and prey. The noises travel back to their ears as echoes, which tell the bats where things are.

Champion of Flying in the Dark

WANDERING ALBATROSS

The wandering albatross has a <u>wingspan</u> of three and a half metres, which makes it the largest seabird in the world. It spends most of its time flying or sitting on the ocean <u>surface</u>.

Champion of Big Wings

It has webbed feet that help it to swim.

Webbed feet

Wandering albatrosses are great at flying. They can glide for hours without stopping for a break. They don't even need to flap their wings.

Champion of Long Flights

They spend the first five or six years of their lives at sea without touching land.

MONARCH BUTTERFLY

Monarch butterflies may be small, but every year millions of them <u>migrate</u> south for warmer weather. Some of them may fly nearly 5,000 kilometres.

Champion of Flying Together

Monarch butterflies eat milkweed, which is usually harmful to other animals. This makes the butterflies taste bad so that <u>predators</u> will not want to eat them.

Milkweed

Champion of Tasting Gross

The monarch butterfly's bright colours warn predators that it is <u>poisonous</u> and will not taste nice.

HOMING PIGEON

Homing pigeons are very good at finding their way home. Scientists are not sure how a homing pigeon knows where to go, but some think they have special senses in their beaks.

Champion of Finding the Way

Scientists also believe that homing pigeons can recognise streets and buildings, which helps them get home.

Homing pigeons are so good at knowing where to go that they have been used by people to send messages home. Pigeons were used in World War One to carry very important messages.

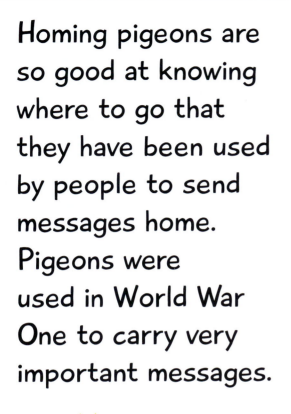

Champion of Sending Mail

Pigeons used to carry messages are sometimes called messenger pigeons or carrier pigeons.

BARN OWL

Barn owls can turn their heads almost all the way around. They cannot move their eyes, so this helps them to see all around them and look out for predators and prey.

Champion of Spinning Around

Barn owls swallow mice and other small animals whole. Their bodies cannot <u>digest</u> the fur, bones and hair of their prey, so they cough up things called pellets.

Champion of Eating Everything

People study owl pellets to find out what things owls have been eating.

COMMON KESTREL

Instead of building a nest of their own for their eggs, kestrels use old nests that other birds have made. They might use an old crow nest, or a nest built from sticks by another bird.

Some kestrels may also settle in nest boxes.

Champion of Sneaky Stealing

Kestrels are very good at hovering. They hover high up in the air to spot their prey. When they see something, they can swoop down quickly to catch it.

When kestrels hover, it means they stay in one place in the air without moving.

Champion of the Hover Hunt

ARCTIC TERN

Arctic terns live in the Arctic for half the year and spend the other half of the year in Antarctica. This is so that they have a whole year of warm, summer weather.

Arctic terns see more sunlight than any other animal on Earth.

Arctic terns fly from the top of the world in the Arctic all the way to the bottom of the world in Antarctica. This is the longest migration of any animal on Earth!

Champion of the Longest Migration

Some Arctic terns fly up to around 70,000 kilometres each year!

Let's see what animal adaptations we humans can use to be champions of the skies!

Use echolocation like a vampire bat and try making echoes in different places.

Flippers are good for swimming, just like an albatross's webbed feet.

You can use a map to find your way like a homing pigeon.

Use a mirror to see behind you just like a barn owl.

23

GLOSSARY

adaptations	changes that have happened to an animal over time and help them to be better suited to their environment
digest	break down into things that can be used by the body
habitats	the natural homes in which animals, plants and other living things live
mammals	animals that have warm blood, a backbone and produce milk
migrate	when animals move from one place to another based on changes in weather
nocturnal	active at night instead of during the day
poisonous	dangerous or deadly when eaten
predators	animals that hunt other animals for food
prey	animals that are hunted by other animals for food
sense	to get information about the world around you, usually by touching, tasting, smelling, seeing or hearing
surface	the uppermost layer
wingspan	the distance from the tip of one wing to the tip of the other

INDEX